VOGGY's HARMONICa BOOK

This is my book:

....

Conception and manuscript: Martina Holtz
Compositions (P. 24, 34, 38, 42, 52, 72, 82, 86): Martina Holtz
Lyrics (P. 58, 68, 80): Martina Holtz

Cover design and illustrations: OZ, Essen (Katrin and Christian Brackmann)

© 2003 Voggenreiter Publishers
Viktoriastr. 25, D-53173 Bonn/Germany
www.voggenreiter.de
info@voggenreiter.de

ISBN: 3-8024-0461-0

Hello!

My name is Voggy and I'll be your musical companion throughout this harmonika book. I'll show you how to play the harmonica with easy explanations, funny drawings and a lot of fun in general. It would be great if your parents could read this book together with you. They could also help you with the little riddles I accidentally dropped somewhere in these pages ...

You'll see me holding a CD alongside many of the songs in this book. This means, you'll find this song on the accompanying CD to play along to. This is explained in further detail on page 94.

One more thing: this book is intended to be used with a standard 10-hole harmonica (also called harp or Blues harp).

Now let's start! I wish you lots of fun with this book and a marvellous time with your harmonica.

Yours musically,
Voggy

Contents

Your Harmonica

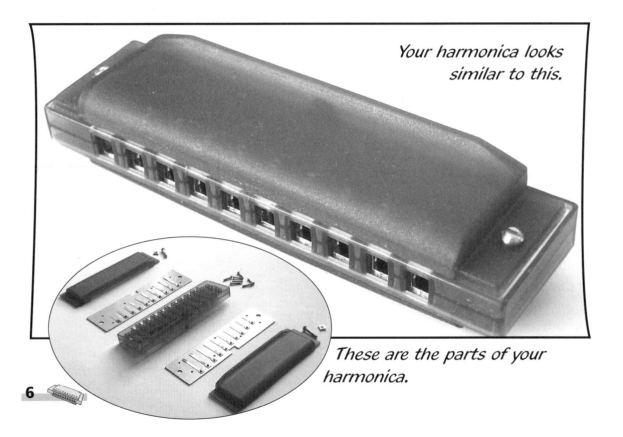

Your harmonica looks similar to this.

These are the parts of your harmonica.

How Sounds Are Produced

As you saw already on page 6, your harmonica has several holes into which you can blow air. We call them **channels** or **air slots**.

You can either blow air through these **channels** (exhale) or draw it in (inhale). The metals strips in the channels vibrate in the stream of air to produce the various sounds.

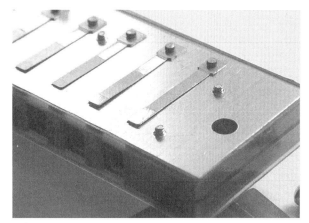

Hold Your Harmonica Like This ...

For a start, use both hands to hold your harp as shown to the left. Keep in mind not to block any of the channels.

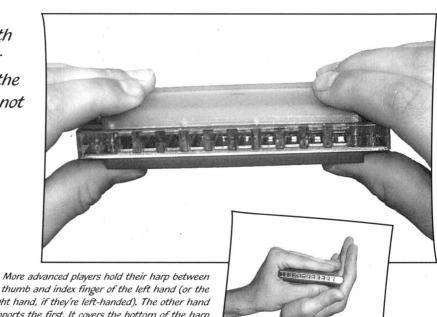

More advanced players hold their harp between thumb and index finger of the left hand (or the right hand, if they're left-handed). The other hand supports the first. It covers the bottom of the harp and is also used for special sound effects and playing techniques.

... Better Not Like This

First Steps Are Easy ...

Just blow gently into your harmonica ...

- *Chances are, you'll be blowing into more than one channel at once, so you'll hear two or more notes simultaneously.*
- *Move your harmonica from left to right: the notes sound lower or higher.*

The low notes are on the left side, the high ones on the right side of your harmonica.

low notes ←——————————————→ high notes

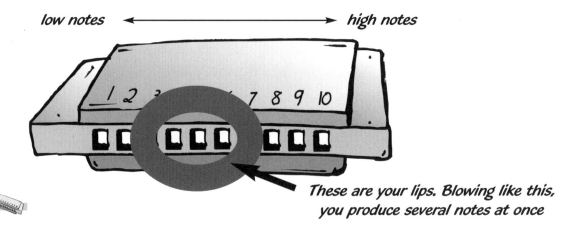

These are your lips. Blowing like this, you produce several notes at once

Kissing Your Harmonica?

Now try blowing into just **one** channel.
You have to make your mouth into a small
oval, similar to giving someone a good-night
kiss on the cheek.

Try this with the other channels, too.

Blow and Draw

As you probably already discovered on your own, you can "blow" into your harmonica as well as "draw" air right through it. These notes are called **blow notes** and **draw notes**, respectively. Every single channel on your harmonica can produce two different pitches or notes, thus making your harmonica a 20-tone instrument (that's not the number of a grand piano, but actually quite enough).

In this book, we'll only use the four middle channels. These are very easy to find: each channel of your harmonica is numbered on top of your instrument. We'll use the channels numbered 4, 5, 6 and 7).

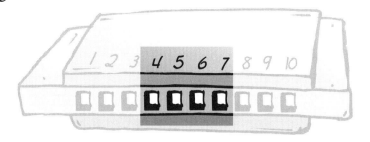

A Little Help

Here's a little hint to make starting easier for you:
Use sticky tape to cover the three channels to the utmost left and the
three channels to the utmost right, so only the middle four remain open
(these are the ones we'll use in this book).
When you've made a little progress later on, you simply remove the
sticky tape.

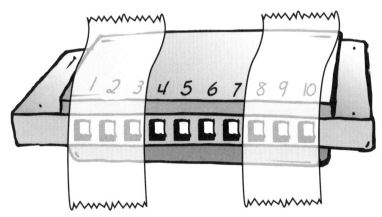

Hooo and Tooo

There are myriads of possibilities to blow into your harmonica.
For a start, try these:

- Blow very gently into your harmonica, like
  breathing a soft "hooo".
- Now use a little more force; more like saying "tooo" into your harmonica.
  Experiment with the force of your blowing to get a feeling for the sound
  produced.

The same holds true for the draw notes: you can play "hooo" and "tooo"
for these on your harmonica, too.

15

Your First Note

The symbol to the left means:

Blow into channel No. 4.

The arrow pointing upwards means to "blow into". The number indicates which channel to blow into. This note is called **C**.

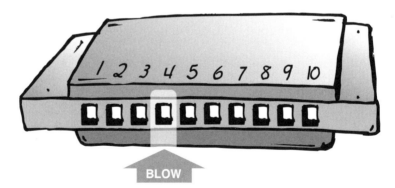

*These symbols are called **tablature**. You read them as you would read a book: from left to right. Say you see something like this:*

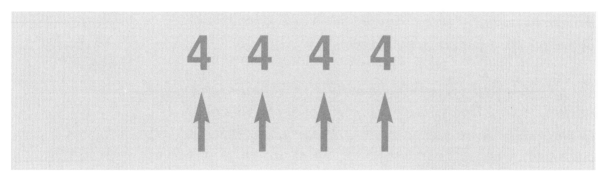

It reads like this: blow four times into channel No. 4.

And Now ... Draw!

An arrow pointing down means:
Draw air through channel No. 4.

Try to use a soft "tooo" for breathing in. Always keep in mind to breathe through your harmonica and not to let any air leave your mouth without going through your harmonica.
This note is called **D.**

Now it's starting to become difficult: we'll play **two** notes.
But relax: we'll use only **one** channel, though.
Look at the graphic below. It shows you what to do:

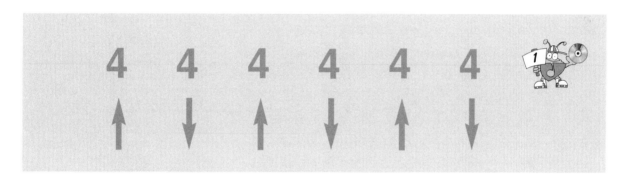

Exactly! **First** you **blow** into channel 4, **then** you **draw** through channel 4.
Repeat the whole thing twice.

Notes

There's a small problem with **tablature**: in music there are long notes as well as short ones. In tablature you can't see whether you're supposed to be playing a long or a short note. To show you what note values to play (how long or how short a note is supposed to sound), there's a system of writing music down called (standard) **notation**. In notation, a symbol called a note is used for every sound you produce (in this book, we'll use standard notation along with tablature, so you'll be learning the best of both worlds).
A note is made up of a note head and a note stem.

This note is called a **quarter note** (or crotchet).

Note stem

Note head

To show you the pitch of the notes, they are written (or "notated") on a so-called **staff**. To show you that these are indeed notes (not subway rails or something else) a so-called **clef** is written at the beginning of the staff. Notes can be written with their note heads on or between the lines. The higher up the note head, the higher the pitch produced (you can imagine the notes standing on the steps of a ladder). Notes are read exactly like (written) words, from left to right.

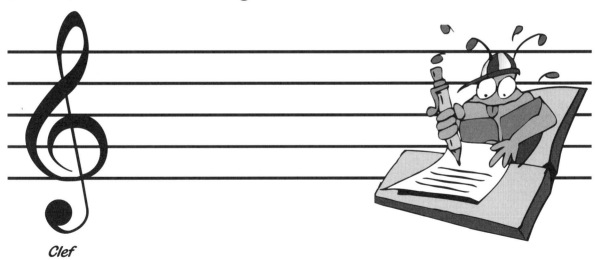

Clef

The Note C

The first note is called C (you already know this one). The sound it produces is so low that it no longer fits on our five lines of the staff. We even have to write a **ledger line** (a little "help" line) for it below the staff.

As a little hint, we'll write the playing symbol above each note so you can see immediately which channel belongs to the note and whether you should draw or blow.

The note C

The Note D

The note D

You already know the note D, too. It is one note higher than C. You'll find it below the bottom line of the staff.

Above the staff, you'll see the tablature symbol for the note D.
It means that you should draw air in through channel 4.

Play It Again, Sam

Here we have the same tones again, written as notes. Above the notes, you'll find the tablature. When you have played the first line to the end, just continue playing at the beginning of the second line...

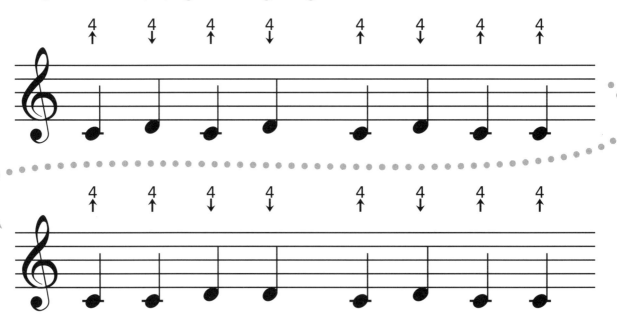

Counting

The last example was very hard to read.
This is why we will now group all the notes into fours.

As a little practice exercise, we'll count to four and then we'll repeat this several times.

1 2 3 4   *1 2 3 4*   *1 2 3 4*   *1 2 3 4*   *etc.*

Clap your hands to each number.

Meter

We'll repeat the exercise from the previous page with notes and this time we'll separate the groups of four with vertical lines. These vertical lines are known as **bar lines**. A group of notes separated by two bar lines is called a **measure** or **bar**.

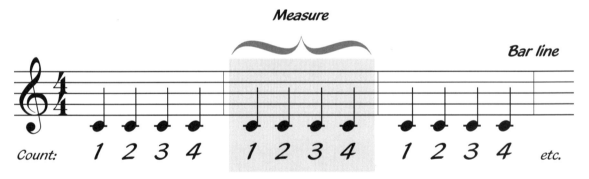

So that we know right from the start that these measures contain groups of four, we write 4/4 at the beginning of the staff. We call this the meter or **time signature**.

This is the tune from page 24 again: this time with bar lines and the meter.

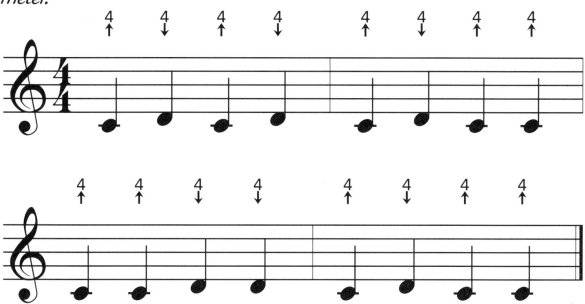

So that we know that we have reached the end of a tune, the last measure is marked with a **final double bar**.

Half Notes (Minims)

The quarter note takes its name from the fact that (just like with a cake) four quarter notes make one whole measure. If you divide the measure into two halves, the resulting notes are called **half notes** (or minims).

The half note is twice as long as the quarter note. It looks similar to a quarter note but with one difference: it has a white, unfilled note head.

 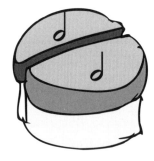

The half note

Take a look at this comparison:

*With the **quarter notes**, you play a note for every number.*

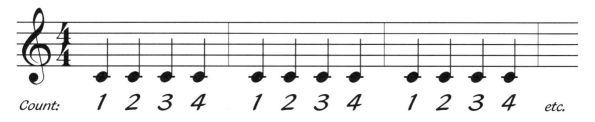

Count: *1 2 3 4   1 2 3 4   1 2 3 4* etc.

*With the **half notes**, every sound you produce lasts for two counts (i.e. two beats):*

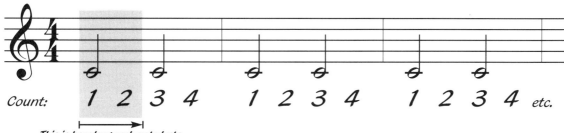

Count: *1 2 3 4   1 2 3 4   1 2 3 4* etc.

This is how long each note lasts.

Play this short piece using one note. Count along silently and make sure the half notes last for two beats.

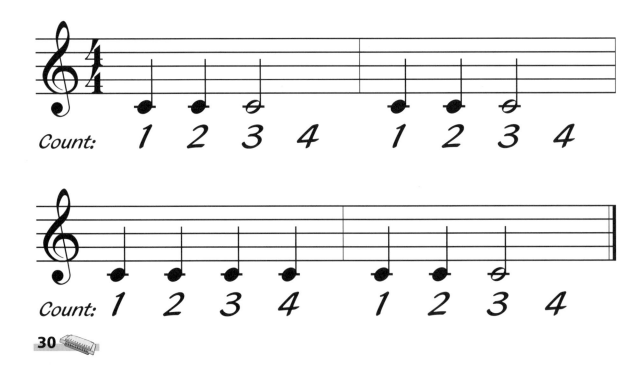

Count: 1 2 3 4 1 2 3 4

Count: 1 2 3 4 1 2 3 4

The Note E

Now it's time for the next channel.
Our third note is E. For this note,
you should blow into channel No. 5.

You'll find the note E
on the bottom line of the staff.
Blow into channel 5.

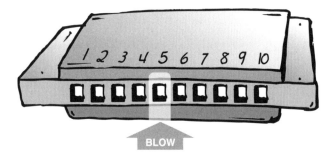

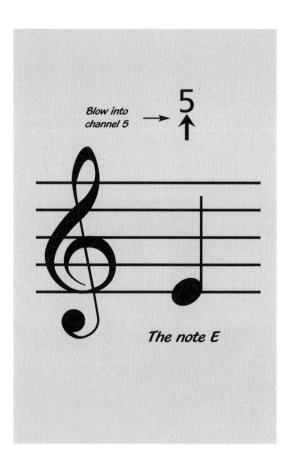

Blow into channel 5 → 5

The note E

Exercise: Play the notes C and E alternately. Move the harmonica to and fro in front of your mouth. As soon as you have reached the new channel, blow "tooo" lightly into the harmonica.

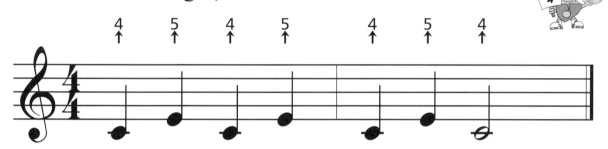

The next exercise is quite difficult:

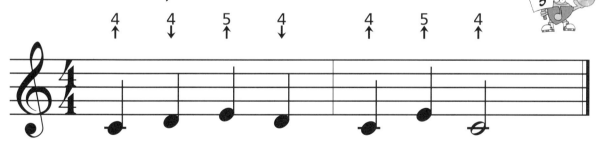

Sleep Tight

Careful! This song spans two pages.

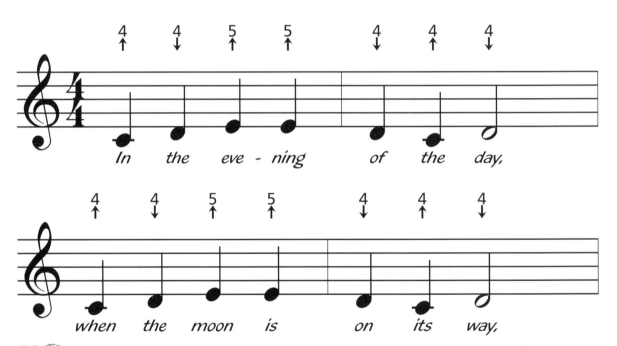

just   sleep   tight,   just   sleep   tight,

just   sleep   tight   my   ba - by   child.

The Note F

To produce the note F, you have to
draw in air through channel 5.
So, as you can see, channel 5 produces both the notes E and F.

You'll find the note F between the
last two lines of the staff.

Draw air into
channel 5

The note F

Still Remember All the Notes?

Write the names of the notes in the boxes.
You'll find the answers on page 92.

Pet's Concert

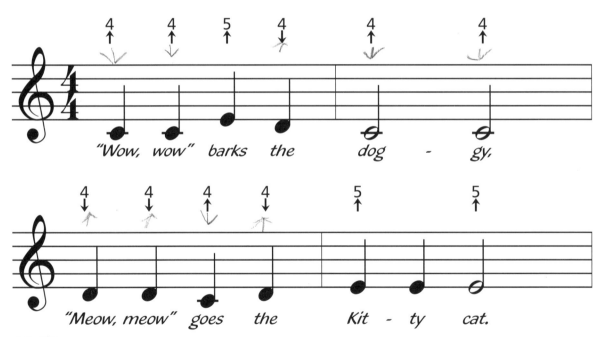

"Wow, wow" barks the dog - gy,

"Meow, meow" goes the Kit - ty cat.

39

Rest a While!

Almost all melodies contain parts where there is no singing or where no instrument is played. We call these parts rests and they are shown in the notation by **rest signs**. The one shown is the **half rest**. It is a very thick stroke and it sits on the third line of the staff. The half rest has the same value as the half note.

Half rest

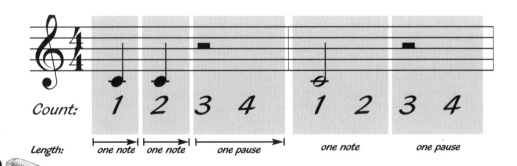

Count: 1   2   3   4   1   2   3   4

Length: one note   one note   one pause   one note   one pause

When you see a rest sign in a song you can take a short rest, but you need to be ready to continue straight away. Keep the harmonica resting on your lips, because the next notes for you to play will soon follow the rest.
Rests are good opportunities for catching your breath when you've run out of air.
Try out this little **exercise**. Count along silently.

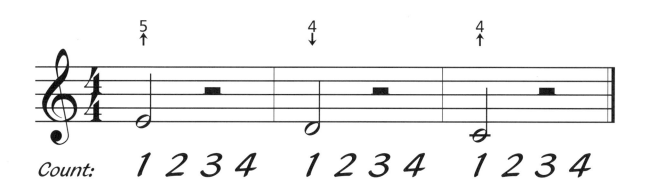

Count: *1 2 3 4   1 2 3 4   1 2 3 4*

One and One

In the second measure, the grey numbers show you how to count.
Play a note on 1 and 2.
Rest on 3 and 4.

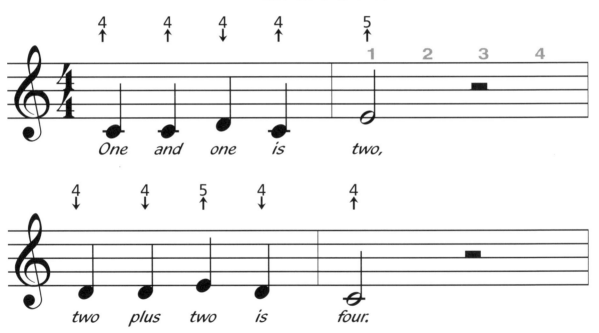

43

The Note G

Once you have mastered G, you will
already know more than half the
notes that you'll meet in this book.
To produce the note G, blow into
channel 6.
You'll find G on the second line from
the bottom of the staff.

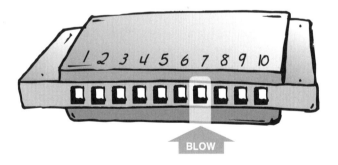

Blow into
channel 6.

The note G

Merrily We Roll Along

The new note only occurs twice in this song.

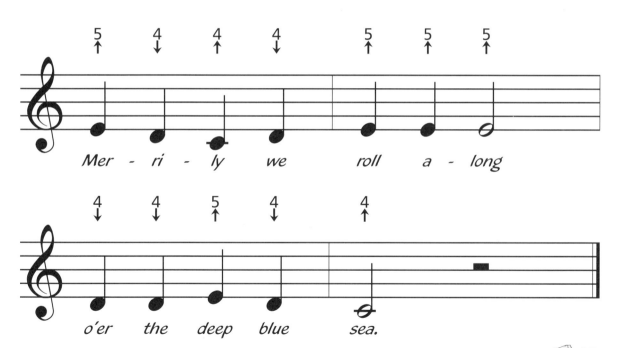

47

Go, Tell Aunt Rhody

This song is really good for practicing all the notes you have learned so far.

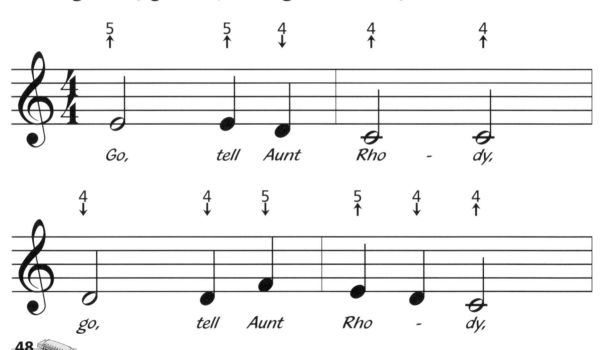

49

A Short Rest!

Quarter rest

The next piece contains a new type of rest: the **quarter rest**.
This rest is easy to recognize on account of its shape. It almost looks as if little Voggy has lain down to sleep right across the lines of the staff.

The quarter rest has exactly the same value as a quarter note. A measure therefore contains exactly the same number of quarter-note rests as quarter notes.

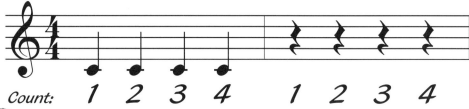

Count: 1   2   3   4   1   2   3   4

Here you see the different notes and rest signs again.
They are also called **note values**.

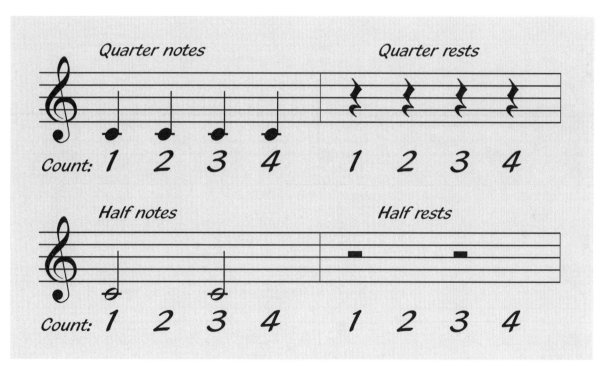

The Monster

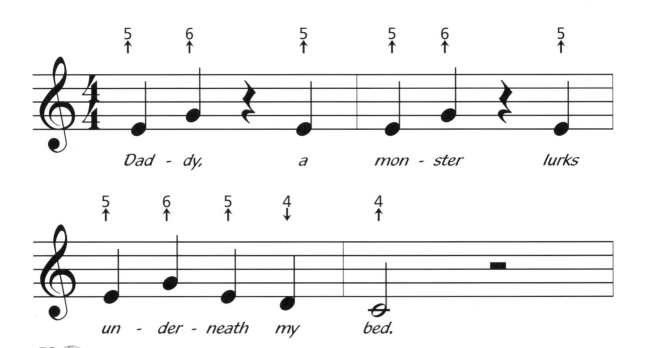

53

Half-time Test

What do we call these symbols?

1.

2.

3.

4.

5. What note does this sign stand for?

 =

6. What note does this sign stand for?

 =

6. What are these notes called?

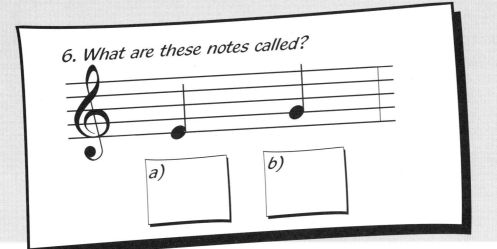

a)

b)

The Note A

Here we have a new note again at last. Draw air through channel 6. You can play both notes G and A on this channel.

You'll find the note A between the second and third lines from the bottom of the staff.

Draw in air through channel 6

The note A

Color this picture!

Bunny in the Meadow

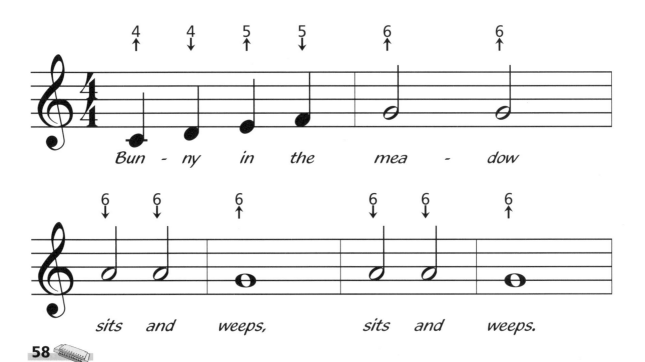

Bun - ny in the mea - dow

sits and weeps, sits and weeps.

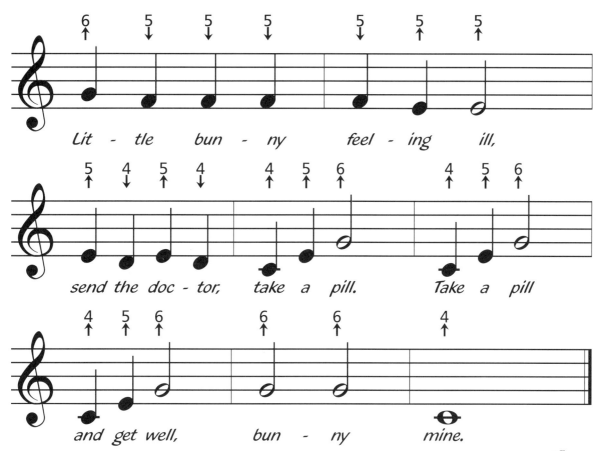

59

London Bridge Is Falling Down

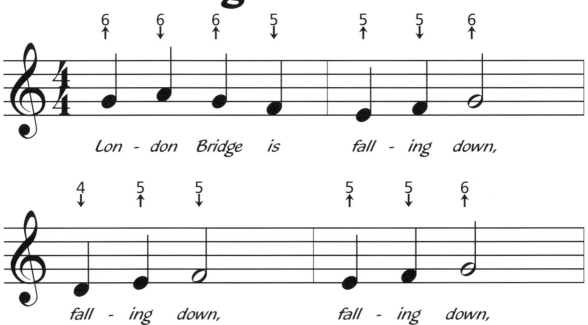

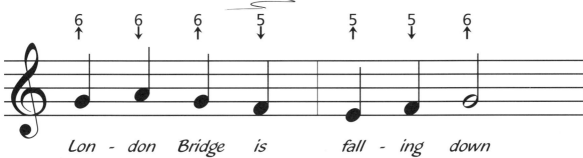

Lon - don Bridge is fall - ing down

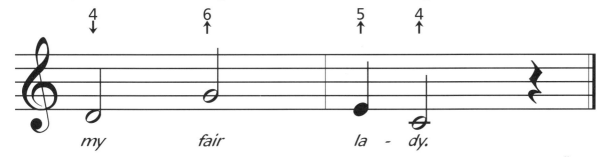

my fair la - dy.

The Measure's Full Now!

The next song contains some notes that last for a whole measure. Such notes are called **whole notes** or semibreves.

The whole note has a white unfilled note head and no stem.

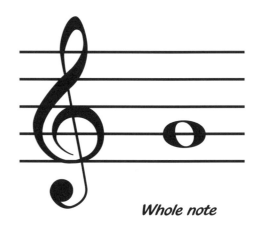

Whole note

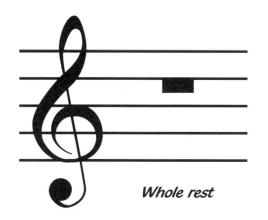

Whole rest

The **whole rest** has exactly the same value as the whole note: one whole measure.

The whole rest is a short bar that hangs below the fourth line of the staff (counting from the bottom). This bar is usually written in the middle of the measure.

Attention! The **whole rest** and the **half rest** look very similar. Compare them well!

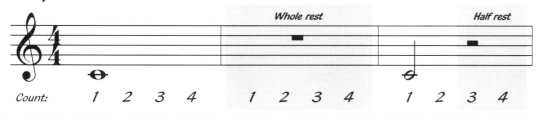

Whole rest   Half rest

Count: 1   2   3   4   1   2   3   4   1   2   3   4

When the Saints Go Marchin' In

Oh, when the saints go mar-ching

in, oh when the saints go

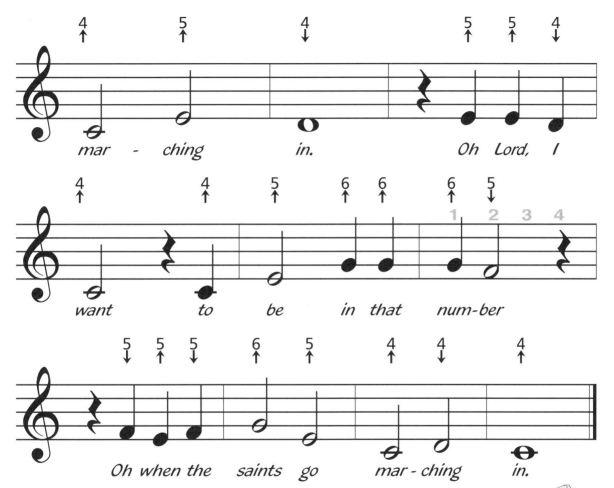

Something's Missing ...

Look at the beginning of the next song. Have you noticed something? Correct. In the first measure there are some notes missing. Instead of containing four quarter notes, there is only one:

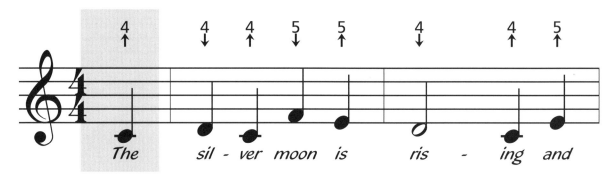

The sil - ver moon is ris - ing and

An incomplete measure at the beginning of a song is called the **upbeat**.

Now take a look at the last measure. There are also some notes missing here because in any song with an upbeat, you add the first measure and the last measure of the song together to produce a whole measure.

First measure   **Last measure**

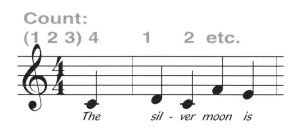

etc.

It's really easy to play an upbeat: You count the measure in the same way you always do (1 2 3 4) but don't start playing until you get to the first note (in this case, the number 4).

The Silver Moon

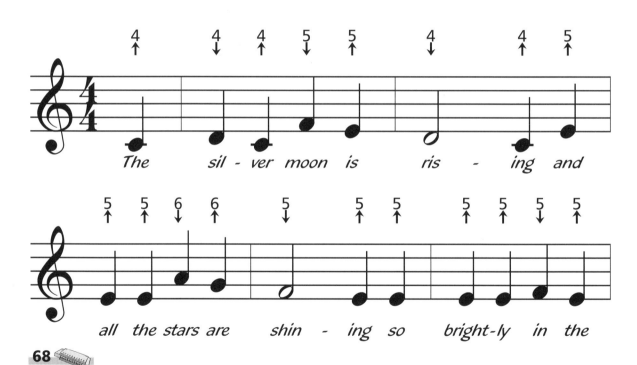

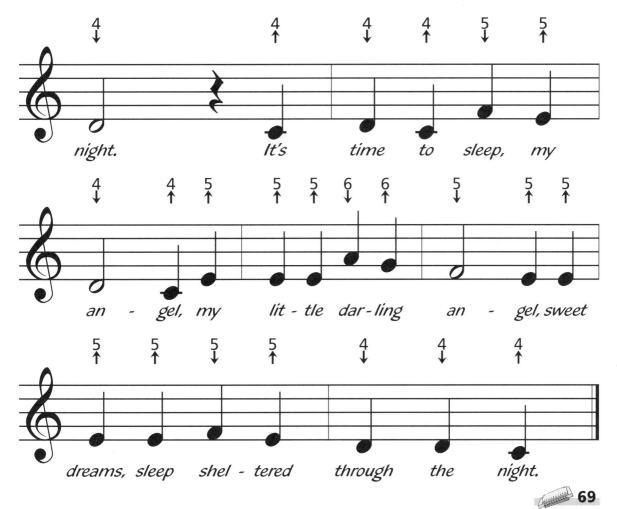

The Note B

The note B is the last note but one that you'll learn in this book.

As you have probably already noticed, this note looks somewhat different to the others because its stem points downwards.

Draw in air through channel 7

The note B

Follow this rule for note stems:
If the head of the note is located on or above the middle line of the staff, the note stem points downwards.

But it's not only the note stem that is different. Until now you had to alternate between drawing and blowing to play all notes one after the other, starting with the lowest and moving to the highest. For the note B you would have had to blow

The note B

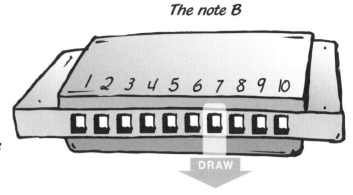

DRAW

again. But on the harmonica we find that the notes for channel 7 have been inverted: For B you actually have to draw in air.

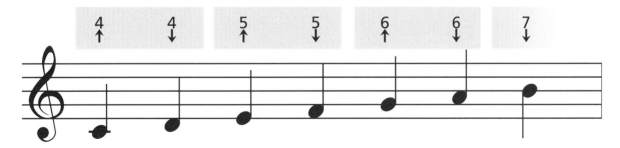

Gingerbread

Gin - ger - bread, gin - ger - bread,

you're my stron - gest wish.

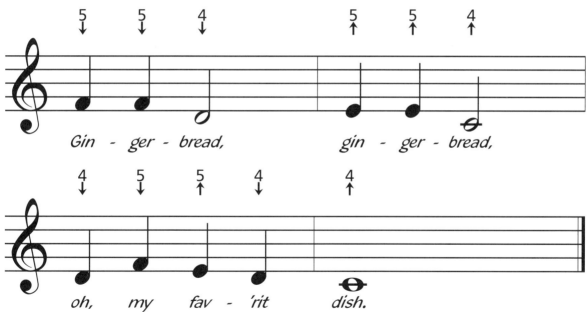

Gin - ger - bread,   gin - ger - bread,

oh,   my   fav - 'rit   dish.

Even Shorter!

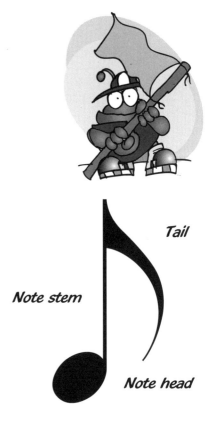

We already know the notes below:

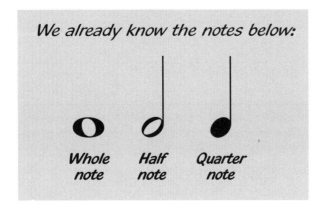

| Whole note | Half note | Quarter note |

Now we can add an even shorter note: the **eighth note** (or quaver). It has a tail attached to its note stem. An eighth note is half the value of a quarter note.

Tail

Note stem

Note head

Eighth note

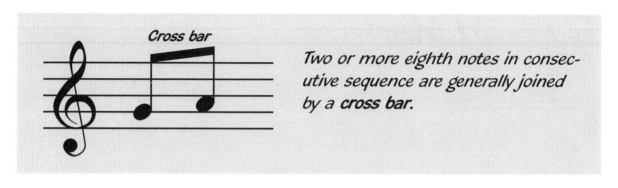

Cross bar

Two or more eighth notes in consecutive sequence are generally joined by a **cross bar.**

Eighth notes are played twice as fast as quarter notes. So that you can play them nice and evenly, count them like this:

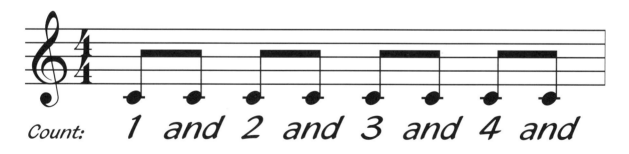

Count: *1 and 2 and 3 and 4 and*

This Old Man

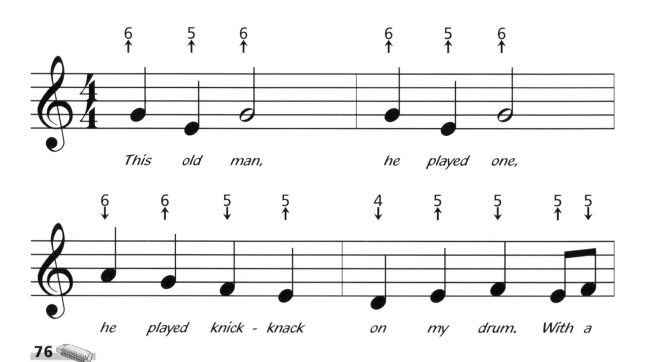

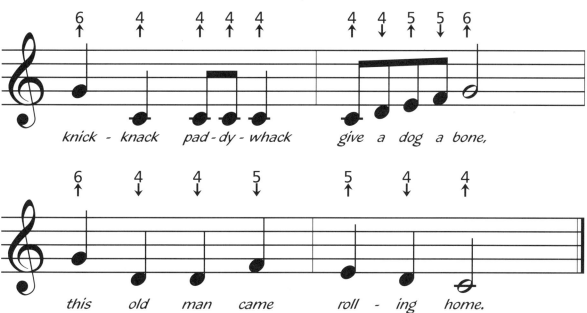

High C

We have already met the note C. But there's also another note called C. Its pitch is twice as high as the other one, which is why we call it "high C".
C is located in the space between the second and third lines from the top of the staff. Its stem points downwards, of course.

High C

This diagram shows you (low) C and high C next to each other.

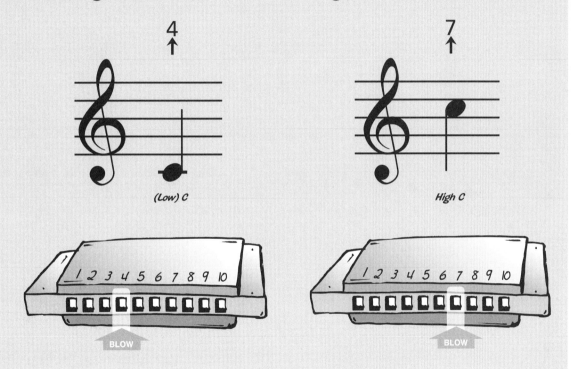

(Low) C

High C

Little Fox

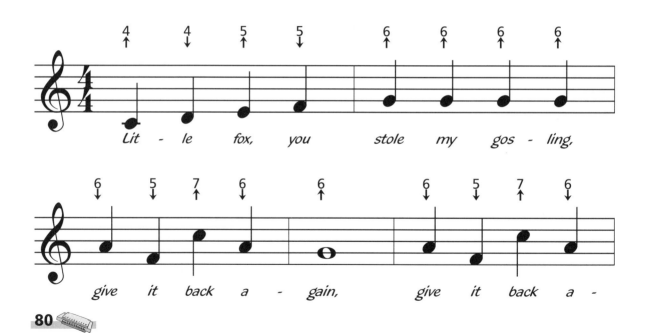

The Cowboy Song

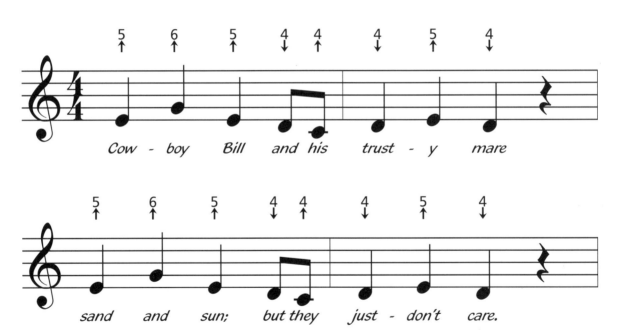

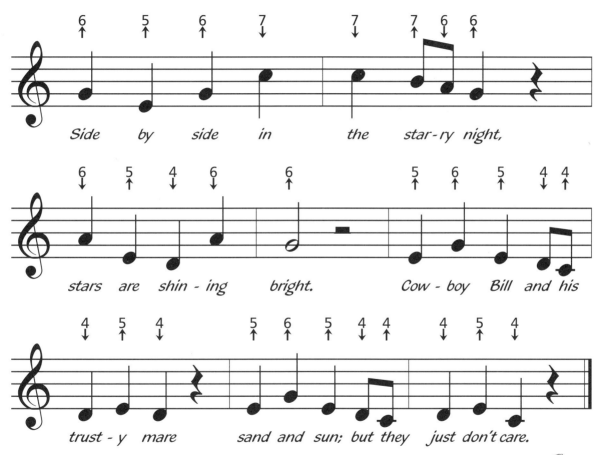

83

Twinkle, Twinkle, Little Star

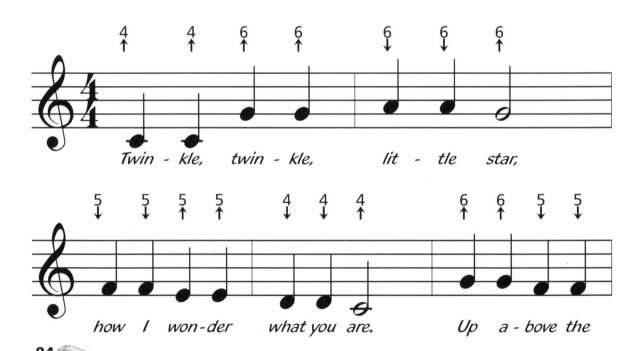

Home Again

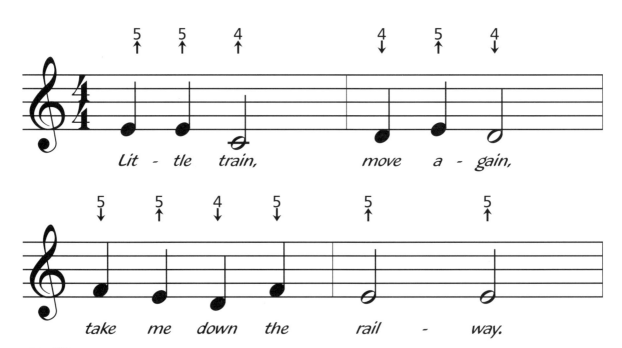

Final Exam

1. What are these notes called?

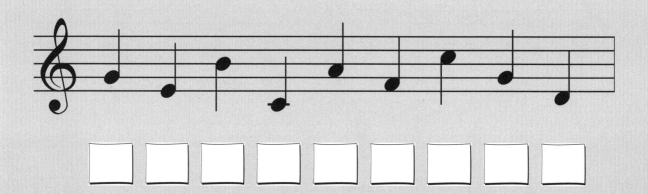

Note and Rest Values

Imagine a measure as being like a cake.

*Four **quarter notes** are like a cake cut into four quarters.*

*Two **half notes** are like a cake cut into two halves.*

*A **whole note** is like a whole cake.*

The Notes on Your Harmonica

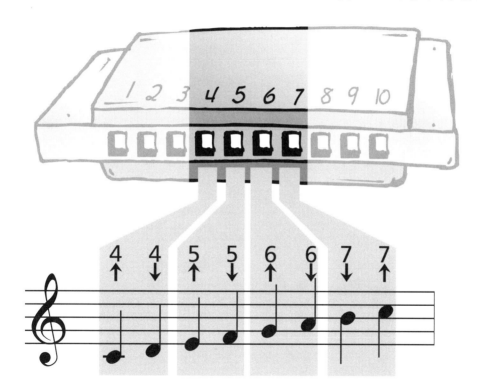

Riddle Solutions

Page 37:   The notes are C, D, E and F.

Page 54:   1. Clef
               2. Quarter note
               3. Half note
               4. Quarter rest
               5. The note D
               6. The note E
               7. a) The note E
                   b) The note G

Page 88:   1. G, E, B, C, A, F, C, G, D
               2. F,   3. E, 4. C, 5. High C,   6. B

Alphabetical Song List

On Using Your CD

All the tunes showing me with a CD in my hand can be found on the CD. I'll hold up a sign to let you know which number.

To make playing along easy, I've recorded every song in three versions, directly following each other:
1. The whole song. This version is for you to listen to and get a general idea of how it's supposed to sound.
2. In this version the melody is played with another sound. You can use it as a "guide" to help you play along.
3. This version only features the accompaniment. Here it's up to you alone to play the melody.

CD Tracks

Voggy's Glockenspiel Book

The glockenspiel simply is one of the best instruments for the first contact with the fascinating world of music. With this book your child will play the first songs after a very short time. Everything you need to know about the basics of music is explained especially for little ones. Therefore, Voggy's Glockenspiel Book is the perfect start to begin a musical education.

DIN A5 landscape format,
ring binding, 80 pages,
with accompanying CD
ISBN 3-8024-0460-2

VOGGY's Recorder Book

No other instrument compares with the recorder for early musical contact. Accompanied by little Voggy, your child will discover this fascinating world, step by step. From the correct way to hold and play the recorder, to learning individual notes, reading music and playing whole tunes. Everything is comprehensively explained in simple terms.

DIN A5 landscape format,
ring binding, 112 pages
ISBN 3-8024-0464-5